Mother Maciag

ideals

EASTER

When earth awakes beneath the touch
    Of Springtime's magic hand,
And April, with her flowery breath
    Comes tripping through the land,
All nature seems to stir and thrill
    With resurrection power,
And buds burst into sudden bloom
    In garden and in bower.

The airy elves so swiftly work
    To change the wintry scene,
I stand amazed to see it clothed
    In garments fresh and green,
And little heralds in the trees
    With lusty voices sing
And tell to all the countryside
    The miracle of spring.

Ralph Meserve

D1406924

Editorial Director, James Kuse

Managing Editor, Ralph Luedtke

Editor/Ideals, Colleen Callahan Gonring

Associate Editor, Linda Robinson

Production Editor/Manager, Richard Lawson

Photographic Editor, Gerald Koser

Copy Editor, Norma Barnes

Art Editor, Duane Weaver

ISBN 0-89542-330-8

IDEALS—Vol. 37 No. 2 February MCMLXXX. IDEALS (ISSN 0019-137X) is published eight times a year,
January, February, April, June, July, September, October, November
by IDEALS PUBLISHING CORPORATION, 11315 Watertown Plank Road, Milwaukee, Wis. 53226
Second class postage paid at Milwaukee, Wisconsin. Copyright © MCMLXXX by IDEALS PUBLISHING CORPORATION.
Postmaster, please send form 3579 to Ideals Publishing Corporation, 175 Community Drive, Great Neck, New York, 11025
All rights reserved. Title IDEALS registered U.S. Patent Office.
Published Simultaneously in Canada.

ONE YEAR SUBSCRIPTION—eight consecutive issues as published—only $15.95
TWO YEAR SUBSCRIPTION—sixteen consecutive issues as published—only $27.95
SINGLE ISSUES—only $2.95

The cover and entire contents of IDEALS are fully protected by copyright and must
not be reproduced in any manner whatsoever. Printed and bound in U.S.A.

Spring Is Here

Walter Edmund Grush

When I gaze out on the landscape,
And nature gives me her glad handshake,
Showing me her work begun,
Her raiment shining in the sun,
Then I know that spring is here,
With winter gone and summer near.

For nothing thrills me so to speak
As growing grass, and flowers meek,
Who bravely force their heads above
The warm brown earth, and gently shove
Away the signs of winter past,
Making way for spring at last.

Why do mortals young and old,
The timid lover, the warrior bold,
Become entranced and dance and play
Like fairy nymphs of yesterday?
They dance and sing with heart that's free,
Throughout the land from sea to sea.

Could it be that Mother Earth
In her great wisdom knows our worth,
And faithfully year after year
Returns to us her children here,
And in us plants the magic seed,
The very impulse that we need?

Spring, a New Beginning

Spring is that long-awaited season that somehow makes the long, cold days of winter seem worthwhile.

It's an anxious creek freeing itself from the icy bonds of winter, tiny tomato seeds pushing sturdy sprouts through rich, black soil on sunny windowsills, and a group of energetic young boys playing baseball on a bare patch of school yard at noon hour.

Spring is a line of patchwork quilts blowing dry in an April breeze, a yardful of newly-arrived robins having an angleworm hunt, and small children happily rediscovering the soggy world that lay beneath the snow.

Spring is a special feeling inside the heart, difficult to define. It's a time of planning, a time of plowing and planting. Spring is a crocus, a green leaf, a pussy willow, a new lamb—and a small child wading light-heartedly through muddy puddles.

Spring brings a bouquet of delightful aromas—the sweet smell of maple syrup cooking over an outside fire; the pungent scent of wood smoke, hazily drifting over a spring-burned meadow; and the fresh fragrance of sheets and pillowcases, line dried on a windy washday.

Spring is a fascinating medley of sounds, eagerly rendered by frogs in a roadside marsh, partridge patiently drumming on an unseen log, songbirds perched high in newly budded treetops, and aeolian chimes constantly changing tempo.

Spring is that time between winter and summer when thoughts of the farmer turn once again to the soil. It is a time of Easter renewal and a time of new life. Spring is a new beginning.

Faye M. Estabrooks

Spring...Today

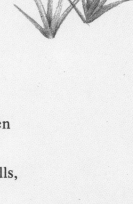

Spring drifts across the land today,
And sunshine melts the snow
On fields where soon a colored rug
Of crocuses will blow.

And tall trees walking up the sky
Perceive it's springtime blue
And start to dress themselves in green
As well-dressed trees should do,

For spring blows down awakened hills,
And vagrant music comes
Where minstrel winds find melodies
To stir the gypsy drums!

Helen Welshimer

Spirit of Spring

Joy is just around the bend,
Spring is on the way.
Need I tell you how I know—
A robin chirped today!

Crocus showed its loveliness,
Tulips came in view,
Down along the woodland stream
Breezes whispered, too!

Joy is just around the bend,
Spring is on the way,
April brought the sunbeams
For my heart today!

Caroline S. Kotowicz

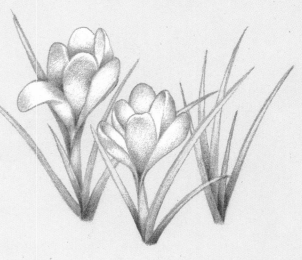

A Thousand Robins

The year was 1811. The place was a little store in the frontier village of Louisville, Kentucky. A handsome young man by the name of John James Audubon was holding a conversation with a certain Alexander Wilson.

"Your ornithology book is very interesting, Mr. Wilson," Audubon said, "but, would you mind taking a look at my collection of birds. I've made them as lifelike as possible."

Alexander Wilson smiled. What could this humble storekeeper possibly know about birds that he did not know? He resented Audubon's confidence, yet he could not contain his curiosity. "Of course, I'd like to see them," Wilson remarked rather sarcastically.

Audubon stooped down under his counter, and a few moments later Alexander Wilson was gazing at some of the most remarkable art work he had ever seen. In fact, they were so amazing that Wilson forgot his disdain completely and did not even pause to envy so great a talent.

"These are the most realistically beautiful paintings I have ever seen, Audubon," he exclaimed, "but why are you hiding them here? Man, you shouldn't be clerking your life away here in this store. Why, you're an artist!"

Audubon laughed. This was not the first man who had enlightened him about his talents. He knew he was an artist, but artists had to eat; and how else could he provide for himself and his wife than by running this little store? Certainly people liked his paintings, but they would not pay him a cent for them. And compliments did not put bread on his table.

"I know I'm no businessman," Audubon said, "but I have no other means of support. Whether I like it or not, I'm forced to stay here and eke out a living. When the store is closed or my wife keeps it, I do my drawings."

"Where did you acquire your mastery, though?" Wilson inquired. "You surely must have attended some school; these are not amateur works. I can see that."

"I studied art in Paris. You see, my foster father was a wealthy sea captain who owned a great deal of land and could afford to send me to school. I still yearn for my days in Paris," Audubon sighed. "It was there I really began to study and paint birds."

"And your foster father encouraged you?"

"Oh, yes, but he died; and before he died, he had a number of financial reverses. At the end I did not inherit a penny. There was nothing left, not a single piece of property."

Wilson was sorry but frank. "To be perfectly honest with you," he said, "I think it would be better if you painted a thousand robins than if you made a thousand dollars."

"Really?"

"Your future is in painting, not in business. The sooner you give up the store, the happier you will be. When you first told me you had paintings you wanted me to see, I doubted very much their ability to exceed my ornithology, but I was mistaken. I am a man who is big enough to admit it."

John James Audubon never forgot these words of Alexander Wilson, for that man was responsible for his entering upon a painting career.

Audubon talked to his wife Lucy that same evening, and she agreed to keep the store while he painted. Later on he also gave lessons in painting, dancing, and fencing. His wife knew he was happy this way, and so she kept on struggling with the store.

If Alexander Wilson started the fire burning, an interview with Charles Bonaparte heaped coals upon it. Bonaparte, nephew of Napoleon, encouraged Audubon to publish his drawings.

The happiest years of the great bird painter's life were between 1827 and 1838. These were the productive years, when he published *The Birds of America*. On both sides of the Atlantic it created a sensation. Lovers of art and science hailed it as a great triumph. There were 435 hand-colored plates, each about three feet high by 2½ feet wide, containing 1,065 pictures of birds, all life-size. All the birds were shown in natural poses. *The Birds of America* cost a small fortune to publish. But always the words of Alexander Wilson came back to him: "It would be better for you to paint a thousand robins than to make a thousand dollars."

It was done, it was finished. He had painted a thousand birds. The world looked at his pictures and agreed with Alexander Wilson.

Lucy Audubon had become a teacher, and her wages financed many of her husband's trips to Europe. After his death in 1851 she continued to teach until she was almost 70.

One of Lucy's former students started an organization called the Audubon Society. Today it is a national organization for bird-watching, with local chapters throughout the United States.

Marion Schoeberlein

© National Audubon Society
Photo from National Audubon Society

A Lovely Day

Good morning, Lord. It's a lovely day.
You ask me how I know?
I can tell by the wind on the crest of the hill
And the morning lights that glow.

I can hear the song of an early bird,
And see the dew on the grass,
And touch the tip of a butterfly wing,
And catch a dream drifting past.

I can breathe the fragrance of the lilac bush,
I can open my lips and sing
And feel the touch of the silent hour,
That only You can bring.

My heart can tell by the feathered clouds,
And the buds on the apple tree.
That's how I know it's a lovely day,
That You have given me.

Thank You, Lord, for a lovely day.

Elsie Claxon Reynolds

Hearty Greetings from Easters Past

EASTER GREETINGS

The flowers lend their colors
Of every varied hue
To brighten up the Easter wish
That Bunny paints for you.

EASTER GREETING

May this Easter message bring
All the beauty of the spring.

May every Easter wish come true
And beauty of the old renew.

May wonders of this Eastertide
Fill hearts with hope, and peace, abide.

May Easter seasons grow more dear
With faith and trust throughout the year.

And may this coming Easter find
Love in the heart of all mankind.

Mamie Ozburn Odum

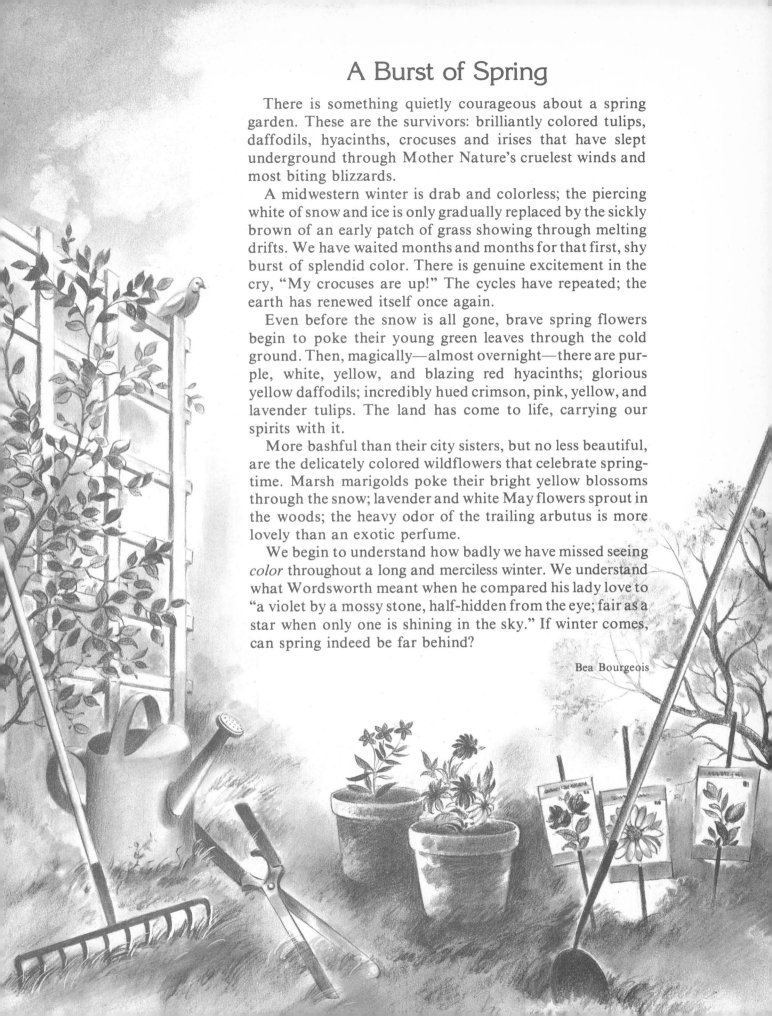

A Burst of Spring

There is something quietly courageous about a spring garden. These are the survivors: brilliantly colored tulips, daffodils, hyacinths, crocuses and irises that have slept underground through Mother Nature's cruelest winds and most biting blizzards.

A midwestern winter is drab and colorless; the piercing white of snow and ice is only gradually replaced by the sickly brown of an early patch of grass showing through melting drifts. We have waited months and months for that first, shy burst of splendid color. There is genuine excitement in the cry, "My crocuses are up!" The cycles have repeated; the earth has renewed itself once again.

Even before the snow is all gone, brave spring flowers begin to poke their young green leaves through the cold ground. Then, magically—almost overnight—there are purple, white, yellow, and blazing red hyacinths; glorious yellow daffodils; incredibly hued crimson, pink, yellow, and lavender tulips. The land has come to life, carrying our spirits with it.

More bashful than their city sisters, but no less beautiful, are the delicately colored wildflowers that celebrate springtime. Marsh marigolds poke their bright yellow blossoms through the snow; lavender and white May flowers sprout in the woods; the heavy odor of the trailing arbutus is more lovely than an exotic perfume.

We begin to understand how badly we have missed seeing *color* throughout a long and merciless winter. We understand what Wordsworth meant when he compared his lady love to "a violet by a mossy stone, half-hidden from the eye; fair as a star when only one is shining in the sky." If winter comes, can spring indeed be far behind?

Bea Bourgeois

My Dear Children,

I am very anxious that you should know something about the history of Jesus Christ, for everybody ought to know about Him. No one ever lived who was so good, so kind, so gentle, and so sorry for all people who did wrong, or were in any way ill or miserable, as He was.

That you may know what the people meant when they said, "Crucify him!" I must tell you that in those times, which were very cruel times indeed (Let us thank God and Jesus Christ that they are past!) it was the custom to kill people who were sentenced to death by nailing them alive on a great wooden cross planted upright in the ground and leaving them there, exposed to the sun and wind, day and night, until they died of pain and thirst. It was the custom, too, to make them walk to the place of execution, carrying the cross-piece of wood to which their hands were to be afterwards nailed, that their shame and suffering might be the greater.

Bearing His cross upon His shoulder, like the commonest and most wicked criminal, Our Blessed Saviour, Jesus Christ, surrounded by the persecuting crowd, went out of Jerusalem to a place called, in the Hebrew language, Golgatha, that is, the place of a skull. And, having come to a hill called Mount Calvary, they hammered cruel nails through His hands and feet and nailed Him on the cross between two other crosses, on each of which a common thief was nailed in agony. Over His head they fastened this writing: "Jesus of Nazareth, the King of the Jews," in three languages, Hebrew, Greek, and Latin.

At about the sixth hour, a deep and terrible darkness came over all the land and lasted until the ninth hour, when Jesus cried out with a loud voice, "My God, my God, why hast Thou forsaken me!" The soldiers, hearing Him, dipped a sponge in some vinegar that was standing there and, fastening it to a long reed, put it up to His mouth. When He had received it, He said, "It is finished!" And crying, "Father! Into Thy hands I commend my spirit!" He died.

The next day being the Sabbath, the Jews were anxious that the bodies should be taken down at once, and made that request to Pilate. Therefore, some soldiers came and broke the legs of the two criminals to kill them; but coming to Jesus and finding Him already dead, they only pierced His side with a spear. From the wound there came out blood and water.

There was a good man named Joseph of Arimathea, a Jewish city, who believed in Christ, and going to Pilate privately (for fear of the Jews) begged that he might have the body. Pilate consenting, he and one Nicodemus rolled it in linen and spices because it was the custom of the Jews to prepare bodies for burial in that way; then they buried it in a new tomb or sepulchre, which had been cut out of a rock in a garden near to the place of crucifixion, and where no one had ever yet been buried. They then rolled a great stone to the mouth of the sepulchre, and left Mary Magdalene, and the other Mary sitting there watching it.

The chief priests and Pharisees, remembering that Jesus Christ had said to His disciples that He would rise from the grave on the third day after His death, went to Pilate and prayed that the sepulchre might be well taken care of until that day, lest the disciples should steal the body, and afterwards say to the people that Christ was risen from the dead. Pilate agreeing to this, a guard of soldiers was set over it constantly, and the stone was sealed up besides. And so it remained, watched and sealed, until the third day, which was the first day of the week.

When that morning began to dawn, Mary Magdalene and the other Mary and some other women, came to the sepulchre, with some more spices which they had prepared. As they were saying to each other, "How shall we roll away the stone?" the earth trembled and shook, and an angel, descending from heaven, rolled it back and then sat resting on it. His countenance was like lightning, and his garments were white as snow; at sight of him the men of the guard fainted away with fear, as if they were dead.

Mary Magdalene ran to Peter and John who were coming towards the place, and said, "They have taken away the Lord and we know not where they have laid Him!" They immediately ran to the tomb. When Peter came up, he went in, and saw the linen clothes lying in one place, and a napkin that had been bound about the head, in another. John also went in, then, and saw the same things. Then they went home, to tell the rest.

But Mary Magdalene remained outside the sepulchre, weeping. After a little time, she stooped down, and looked in, and saw two angels, clothed in white, sitting where the body of Christ had lain. These said to her, "Woman, why weepest thou?" She answered, "Because they have taken away my Lord, and I know not where they have laid Him." As she gave this answer, she turned round, and saw Jesus standing behind her, but did not then know Him. "Woman," said He, "why

weepest thou? What seekest thou?" She, supposing Him to be the gardener, replied, "Sir! If thou hast borne my Lord hence, tell me where thou hast laid Him, and I will take Him away." Jesus pronounced her name, "Mary." Then she knew Him, and, starting, exclaimed, "Master!" "Touch me not," said Christ, for I am not yet ascended to my Father; but go to my disciples, and say unto them, I ascend unto my Father, and your Father, and to my God, and to your God!"

Accordingly, Mary Magdalene went and told the disciples that she had seen Christ, and what He had said to her; and with them she found the other women whom she had left at the sepulchre when she had gone to call those two disciples, Peter and John. These women told her and the rest that they had seen at the tomb two men in shining garments, at sight of whom they had been afraid, and had bent down, but who had told them that the Lord was risen; and also that as they came to tell this, they had seen Christ, on the way, and had held Him by the feet, and worshipped Him. But these accounts seemed to the apostles, at that time, as idle tales, and they did not believe them.

The soldiers of the guard too, when they recovered from their fainting fit and went to the chief priests to tell them what they had seen, were silenced with large sums of money and were told by them to say that the disciples had stolen the body away while they were asleep.

But it happened that on that same day, Simon and Cleopas, Simon one of the twelve apostles and Cleopas one of the followers of Christ, were walking to a village called Emmaus, at some little distance from Jerusalem, and were talking by the way upon the death and resurrection of Christ, when they were joined by a stranger, who explained the Scriptures to them and told them a great deal about God, so that they wondered at His knowledge. As the night was fast coming on when they reached the village, they asked this stranger to stay with them, which He consented to do. When they all three sat down to supper, He took some bread, and blessed it, and broke it as Christ had done at the Last Supper. Looking on Him in wonder they found that His face was changed before them, and that it was Christ Himself; and as they looked at Him, He disappeared.

They instantly rose up, and returned to Jerusalem, and, finding the disciples sitting together, told them what they had seen. While they were speaking, Jesus suddenly stood in the midst of all the company, and said, "Peace be unto you." Seeing that they were greatly frightened, He showed them His hands and feet, and invited them to touch Him.

But Thomas, one of the twelve apostles, was not there at that time; and when the rest said to him afterwards, "We have seen the Lord!" he answered, "Except I shall see in His hands the print of the nails, and thrust my hand into His side, I will not believe!" At that moment, though the doors were all shut, Jesus again appeared, standing among them, and said, "Peace be unto you!" Then He said to Thomas, "Reach hither thy finger, and behold my hands; and reach hither thy hand, and thrust it into my side; and be not faithless, but believing." And Thomas answered, and said to Him, "My Lord and my God!" Then said Jesus, "Thomas, because thou hast seen me, thou hast believed. Blessed are they that have not seen me, and yet have believed."

After that time, Jesus Christ was seen by five hundred of His followers at once, and He remained with others of them forty days, teaching them, and instructing them to go forth into the world and preach His gospel and religion, not minding what wicked men might do to them. And conducting His disciples at last out of Jerusalem as far as Bethany, He blessed them, and ascended in a cloud to heaven, and took His place at the right hand of God. And while they gazed into the bright blue sky where He had vanished, two white-robed angels appeared among them, and told them that as they had seen Christ ascend to heaven, so He would, one day, come descending from it, to judge the world.

When Christ was seen no more, the Apostles began to teach the people as He had commanded them. And through the power He had given them they healed the sick, and gave sight to the blind, and speech to the dumb, and hearing to the deaf, as He had done. They took the name of Christians from Our Saviour, Christ.

Remember! It is Christianity to do good, always, even to those who do evil to us. It is Christianity to love our neighbours as ourself, and to do to all men as we would have them do to us. It is Christianity to be gentle, merciful, and forgiving, and to keep those qualities quiet in our own hearts, and never make a boast of them, or of our prayers or of our love of God, but always to show that we love Him by humbly trying to do right in everything. If we do this, and remember the life and lessons of Our Lord Jesus Christ, and try to act up to them, we may confidently hope that God will forgive us our sins and mistakes, and enable us to live and die in peace.

Charles Dickens

Small Downy Things

A touch of fur wraps newborn things
Especially in early spring,
As if some higher power knew
That north winds bite and storms chill through.

Beside the brook, the willow tree
Is wearing fur quite tastefully,
For pussy willows lift a head
While ice still skims the riverbed.

The meadow struts in puffs of gold—
A breathless beauty to behold.
Spread helter-skelter in design
Are scads and scads of dandelion.

Where trim, white fences skirt the land,
Soft fuzzy colts try hard to stand.
Sheep graze content down by the pump
While woolly lambs gambol and jump.

A chanticleer gives out his sound.
The barnyard group must scurry round
With clucking calls and scratchy tricks.
They teach the fluffy ducks and chicks.

Soft bunnies hop and scurry by,
Or stop and look you in the eye.
God certainly loved the world in spring;
He filled it with small downy things.

Alice Leedy Mason

The Tale of Peter Rabbit

Once upon a time there were four little rabbits, and their names were Flopsy, Mopsy, Cottontail, and Peter. They lived with their mother in a sandbank, underneath the root of a very big fir tree.

"Now, my dears," said old Mrs. Rabbit one morning, "you may go into the fields or down the lane, but don't go into Mr. McGregor's garden. Your father met with an accident there; he was put in a pie by Mrs. McGregor. Now run along, and don't get into mischief. I am going out."

Then old Mrs. Rabbit took a basket and her umbrella, and went through the woods to the baker's. She bought a loaf of bread and five currant buns.

Flopsy, Mopsy, and Cottontail, who were good little bunnies, went down the lane to gather blackberries; but Peter, who was very naughty, ran straight away to Mr. McGregor's garden, and squeezed under the gate! First he ate some lettuces and some French beans; and then he ate some radishes; and then, feeling rather sick, he went to look for some parsley.

But round the end of a cucumber frame, whom should he meet but Mr. McGregor.

Mr. McGregor was on his hands and knees planting young cabbages, but he jumped up and ran after Peter, waving a rake and calling out, "Stop thief!"

Peter was most dreadfully frightened; he rushed all over the garden, for he had forgotten the way back to the gate. He lost one of his shoes among the cabbages, and the other shoe among the potatoes.

After losing them, he ran on four legs, and went faster, so that I think he might have gotten away altogether, if he had not unfortunately run into a gooseberry net, and got caught by the large buttons on his jacket. It was a blue jacket with brass buttons, quite new.

Peter gave himself up for lost, and shed big tears; but his sobs were overheard by some friendly sparrows, who flew to him in great excitement, and implored him to exert himself.

Mr. McGregor came up with a sieve, which he intended to pop upon the top of Peter; but Peter wriggled out just in time, leaving his jacket behind him.

He rushed into the tool shed, and jumped into a can. It would have been a beautiful thing to hide in, if it had not had so much water in it.

Mr. McGregor was quite sure that Peter was somewhere in the tool shed, perhaps hidden underneath a flowerpot. He began to turn them over carefully, looking under each.

Presently Peter sneezed—"kertyschoo!" Mr. McGregor was after him in no time. And he tried to put his foot upon Peter, who jumped out the window, upsetting three plants. The window was too small for Mr. McGregor, and he was tired of running after Peter. He went back to his work.

Peter sat down to rest; he was out of breath and trembling with fright, and he had not the least idea which way to go. Also he was very damp from sitting in that can.

After a time he began to wander about, going lippity-lippity not very fast, and looking all around.

Then he tried to find his way straight across the garden, but he became more and more puzzled. Presently he came to a pond where Mr. McGregor filled his water cans. A white cat was staring at some goldfish. She sat very, very still, but now and then the tip of her tail twitched as if it were alive. Peter thought it best to go away without speaking to her; he had heard about cats from his cousin, little Benjamin Bunny.

He went back toward the tool-shed, but suddenly, quite close to him, he heard the noise of a hoe—scr-r-ritch, scratch, scratch, scritch. Peter scuttered underneath the bushes. But presently, as nothing happened, he came out, and climbed upon a wheelbarrow and peeped over. The first thing that he saw was Mr. McGregor hoeing onions. His back was turned toward Peter, and beyond him was the gate.

Peter got down very quietly off the wheelbarrow, and started running as fast as he could go, along a straight walk behind some black currant bushes. Mr. McGregor caught sight of him at the corner, but Peter did not care. He slipped underneath the gate, and was safe at last in the woods outside the garden.

Mr. McGregor hung up the little jacket and the shoes for a scarecrow to frighten the blackbirds.

Peter never stopped running or looked behind him till he got home to the big fir tree. He was so tired that he flopped down upon the nice, soft sand on the floor of the rabbit hole, and shut his eyes. His mother was busy cooking; she wondered what he had done with his clothes. It was the second little jacket and pair of shoes that Peter had lost in a fortnight!

I am sorry to say that Peter was not very well during the evening. His mother put him to bed and made some camomile tea; and she gave a dose of it to Peter!

"One tablespoonful to be taken at bed-time."

But Flopsy, Mopsy, and Cottontail had bread and milk and blackberries, for supper.

Beatrix Potter
1886-1943

THE TALE OF PETER RABBIT by Beatrix Potter, reproduced by permission of the publisher, Frederick Warne & Company, Inc.

Easter Is a Constant Spring

Easter is a reminding time . . .
Of colored eggs and pretty dresses,
Of yellow chicks and curly tresses.

Easter is a renewing time . . .
For baby bunnies, birds, and bees,
For sun and rain on budding trees.

Easter is a grateful time . . .
For all our blessings every day,
For health and friends along the way.

Easter is a believing time . . .
That Christ arose for us to see
The way to grow eternally.

Easter is a joyful time . . .
For thoughts, for growth, for songs to sing.
Yes, Easter is a constant spring.

Ruth Carrington

Two Mothers

Two mothers sat neath an olive tree
　　Discussing their sons very earnestly.
One woman said, and her head was held proud,
　　"Our sons are both handsome; they stand out in a crowd."
The other assented and said with a sigh,
　　"How they have grown as years hasten by.
I can recall when my son was a lad
　　He strayed from our group—far from me and his dad.

"We feared we had lost him and traced our steps once again;
　　We discovered him questioning some very learned men.
We scolded him sharply and told him that we
　　Were frantic and worried, complaining that he
Must stay with his friends, not stray and forget.
　　His answer amazed us; he had no regret.
He spoke like a "father"—not a son of our own;
　　I'll always remember even though he is grown."

A smile, oh, so slight, crossed the face of the other,
  "I do understand; it's so hard for a mother.
My Judas is clever, alert and quite bright,
  He handles his money with shrewdest insight.
He's also successful in practising skills
  Of being a leader; he bends people's wills;
Dynamic, magnetic, ambitious is he,
  He strengthens the pride of his father and me."

The first woman shaded her eyes with her shawl,
  "My son isn't interested in money at all!
He'd rather be sailing the rough Galilee
  Or gathering the children round about on his knee.
Although he is gentle, he's very brave too;
  He has steadfastness, firmness, a purpose to do.
He says what he means, and he quotes only Truth
  To rich men and beggars, the old and youth."

The sun blazed on hotter, and both women thought
  They had better bring back the water they sought.
So each mother lifted a jug to her head
  And smiled with affection. Then one of them said,
"It was nice to have met you, since our boys are good friends."
  The other smiled sadly, "Sometimes I wonder how it all ends."

Norma Nolan Santangelo

Eastertime

The dawn awakens in my heart
  As spring first comes to earth,
And then I know 'tis Eastertime
  The glorious rebirth.

The winter fades and disappears
  Along with glistening snow,
And birds begin to sing a song
  Where violets start to grow.

The woodlands bring a message clear
  As blossoms burst in bloom,
And everywhere along life's road
  We hear spring's happy tune.

A song of April fills our hearts
  Midst greening hills sublime.
The skies are blue, the world's alive.
  'Tis blessed Eastertime.

Garnett Ann Schultz

A Prayer for Spring

Brood over the earth, Great Spirit of God,
  With Your wind and Your sun and Your rain;
Thaw out the streams and awaken the sod
  And send us the springtime again.

Back from the southland, send us the songbirds:
  Bluebird and robin, thrasher, and wren.
Send growth to our fields, replenish our herds,
  Smile on our gardens, and then—

Great Spirit and Friend, guard well this good earth,
  For the days and the nights are Your Own.
Thou art their Creator: Thou givest them birth—
  Let all of Thy seasons be known.

Minnie Klemme

And when he had called unto him his twelve disciples,
he gave them power.   Matthew 10:1

Jesus Christ

Christ went about through city and village
Healing the sick and preaching the gospel.
Great truths were explained from another age.
The scrolls in their synagogues He knew well.
Diseases were healed and devils cast out,
But when the dumb spoke, clear as a bell,
The listening crowd marvelled, crying aloud,
"It was never so seen in Israel."

He looked on the multitude and His heart
Moved with compassion. He saw how they came
Following—fainting—standing apart—
Hoping for a miracle in God's name.

Christ saw the need, so much work to do.
"The harvest is great, but the laborers few."

So He called to him twelve, gave them power
And sent them forth, giving instructions as well:
Go not into the way of the Gentiles at this hour,
Go ye to the lost sheep of Israel.
What I tell you in darkness, speak in light.
Are not two sparrows sold for a small amount?
They cannot fall beyond the Father's sight.
The hairs on your head are known to His count.

Other rules He gave to console and relieve.
Knowing well that man is easily led,
He cautioned them—Be not faithless. Believe!
Last of all, speaking tenderly, He said,

"For I send you forth as sheep among wolves.
Be wise as serpents and harmless as doves."

We are pleased to share with you religious Easter selections comprised of poetry and prose. Found within this section are presentations of the Apostles of Jesus Christ: poetry from Alice Leedy Mason; art by Roland Bailey. We have also included excerpts from Ideals publications NORMAN VINCENT PEALE: *The Man, His Ministry* by Richard Lewis Detrich and *To Jerusalem, with Love* by Nat Olson. The Olson article is beautifully illustrated with a painting of Christ before the crowds, *"Ecce Home!"* by Danish painter Henrik Krock. In addition, a painting by Bianchi powerfully portrays the Crucifixion. We hope you will find this section a source of inspiration.

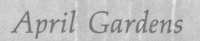

April Gardens

How fitting it was that April night,
To have brought Him back where a garden lay,
Cool and sweet in the early dusk
After a strange and terrible day.

How fitting that out of the dust of the years,
Up from a garden bed should rise
The white, the pure, the everlasting,
Beautiful flower of the skies.

How fitting that gardens everywhere
Recall Him today, His form, His face;
He walks there still in the evening light;
He moves through the morning's shadowy lace.

More radiant, far, than the first white flower,
Or the quivering light of a blossoming bough.
Deep in the gardens of any land,
Those who seek Him may find Him now.

Grace Noll Crowell

*Now the names of the twelve apostles are these: the first, Simon, who is called Peter,
and Andrew his brother; James the son of Zebedee, and John his brother;
Philip and Bartholomew; Thomas, and Matthew the publican;
James the son of Alpheus and Lebbeus, whose surname was Thaddeus;
Simon the Canaanite, and Judas Iscariot, who also betrayed him.*

Matthew 10:2-4

Peter

*Peter was blessed with great physical strength.
Big, strong hands had hauled the nets from the sea.
At the Lord's command, he became at length
A fisher of men for eternity.
Still, he said the wrong things, did the wrong things,
Often came up short when put to the test.
Christ saw more than strength. He saw faith that brings
In the potter's hands, the mark of the best.*

*Peter, that impetuous fisherman,
Is the favorite of many because
His life was a constant struggle to win.
Understanding, they give him great applause.*

*How human were his faults, how well he knew
That the God of all Grace will strengthen you.*

Andrew

*The first of twelve, it was Andrew who came
To see the Messiah, eager to learn
To walk the straight road in the Savior's name.
Convinced by the prophet John, his concern
Was for others—for Simon, his brother.
They grew up together near Galilee,
Heard of the Promised One from their mother.
For them the promise was reality.*

*Later 'twas Andrew who found a young lad
With loaves and fishes, and the hungry were fed.
Always so helpful, he made others glad.
"I will make you fishers of men," Christ said.*

*And Andrew was first, a man set apart,
A true disciple with love in his heart.*

James, the Greater

James was the silent disciple who walked
Close to the Savior with Peter and John.
Though he never spoke out, others who talked
Found him a disciple to depend on.
Lean and bronzed, strong, straight son of Zebedee,
Whose mother became a disciple, too,
Slept on through the prayers of Gethsemane,
Was rudely rejected for being a Jew.

Christ called James and John "The Sons of Thunder."
He rebuked them when they sought to be first.
But it was James who saw Christ's deeds of wonder
And heard Him plead on the cross, "I thirst."

A martyr for Christ, his words fill no pages.
His silence speaks out, down through the ages.

John

John, a fisherman born in Bethsaida,
Was the greatest disciple of all.
Years of sailing rough waters had made a
Strong follower, one on whom Christ could call.
His depth of faith and good understanding
Helped when he wrote of Christ and the times they shared—
Of outdoor life that was so demanding—
Spiritual words telling how much God cared.

John stood at the cross with Mary weeping,
Thinking all they had worked for was done.
Then love so enduring from Heaven came sweeping.
Christ whispered, "Woman, behold thy son!"

In age John grew gentle, to all men a brother.
He prayed, "Little children, love one another."

*The following excerpt
is taken from NORMAN VINCENT PEALE
The Man, His Ministry
By Richard Lewis Detrich*

This Is Norman Vincent Peale

. . . In an average week Peale speaks three or four times in cities scattered across the country, sometimes speaking in one city in the morning and in another, several thousand miles away, the same evening. Each year Peale logs over one hundred fifty thousand air miles. . . .

Peale was born in 1898. Now in his eighties, he keeps a schedule that would leave most younger men exhausted! Few people, certainly not the members of the church or even close associates, can fully comprehend the vastness of Peale's outreach and ministry and the demands placed on him. Everyone wants "just a minute" of Peale's time and when you are "minister to millions" there just aren't enough minutes to go around. . . .

To understand Peale you have to understand what he calls his "jobs." His oldest job, and the one that means the most to him, is as minister of Marble Collegiate Church. The Collegiate Church was begun in 1628 shortly after the Dutch settled the island which was brought from the Manhatoe Indians and is not just one church, but a collective of several worshiping congregations in which all the ministers are colleagues. All of these churches share a common Consistory, or board of directors, and pool their resources. Although Peale came to pastor Marble Collegiate Church in 1932, it was not until 1973 that he actually became the Senior Minister of the Collegiate Church. . . .

Peale is still actively involved in the life and ministry of Marble Collegiate Church. Except during the summer months and January, Peale preaches each Sunday at the 11:15 A.M. service at Marble. The actual administration of the day to day operation of the church has for many years been controlled more by the spirit of Norman Peale than by his person and presence. He has had to rely on carefully selected and trusted associates to run the operation of the church and meet the pastoral needs of the Marble congregation. . . .

Peale and his wife are co-publishers of *Guideposts* magazine and are actively involved in the management of *Guideposts.* "Together we run the business of *Guideposts,*" says Peale. "I'm president, Ruth's executive vice-president. She and I are co-publishers. Whenever we have a board meeting, or an operating meeting, we're both there. We employ about five hundred people at *Guideposts.* . . .

The "speaking business" is another major Peale endeavor. Two or three days every week frequently accompanied by Ruth, Peale is out criss-crossing the country speaking to packed houses at conventions and sales meetings. He cannot possibly accept all the invitations and opportunities to speak which are extended to him and must decline several for each one accepted. . . .

Another Peale "job" is his weekly, syndicated newspaper column "There's an Answer!" which appears in seven hundred newspapers across the country with a total readership of twenty-seven million people!

A more recent Peale "job" is "The American Character," a nationally syndicated radio program broadcast three hundred times a day on a hundred and eighty-five radio stations across the country. "The American Character" is funded by ITT and aims at counterbalancing the media emphasis on what is wrong with our society through daily ninety second reports about what is right with Americans. Each broadcast, narrated by Dr. Peale, focuses on a vignette of modern day American goodness and courage.

There are other Peale jobs. Peale's messages are taped on television and are syndicated across the country. Cassette tapes of his sermons are distributed by the Foundation for Christian Living. He and Ruth serve on many boards of directors. Until recently Peale was chairman of the Horatio Alger Awards Committee. He serves on the board of Central College in Pella, Iowa, and Ruth is on the board of Hope College, Holland, Michigan, both schools of the Reformed Church in America.

Probably Peale's best-known "job" is as a writer. He's written twenty-one books and co-authored two others. His best-known work *The Power of Positive Thinking* has sold over ten million copies in thirty three languages. . .

The Peales' work requires a great deal of travel, but if there is any hobby that they have, it's probably also travel. Ruth says, "Perhaps the greatest benefit in travel is the stimulus of novelty. As you move about, you meet new people, you encounter new ideas, observe new customs, hear new stories. For Norman and me, these experiences are not only stimulating in themselves, they supply the raw material that Norman draws on for radio talks and sermons, lectures and newspaper columns all through the winter months. Many people, I'm sure, think of a writer as someone who, like a kind of human spider, spins his webs out of a magical and inexhaustible reservoir inside him. But this isn't so. You have to take in something before you can send it back out. The creative process that receives this 'something' reshapes it, gives it form and substance and drama. But there has to be a steady input, or the well will run dry."

The Antonia, Where Jesus Was Tried

"When Pilate therefore heard that saying, he brought Jesus forth, and sat down by the judgment seat in a place that is called the Pavement, but in the Hebrew, Gabbatha" (John 19:13).

When I visited the Fort of Antonia, where Jesus was tried, I was gripped with the realization that it was here they mocked and ridiculed my blessed Lord and Savior; it was here they beat him with cruel whips until his very flesh was laid open. One can almost visualize Pilate coming to this central court to adjudicate, speaking the words *"Ecce Homo!"*—"Behold the Man!"

Visitors can still see stones scratched with the games the Roman soldiers played. (There were 500 to 600 Roman soldiers in this one cohort.) The actual pavement was discovered earlier in the twentieth century below the Ecce Homo Convent which is built on the site.

Herod the Great constructed the Antonia by rebuilding an old Maccabean fortress and naming it for Mark Antony. Christ appeared here because the Sanhedrin—Jewish court which had tried Jesus—could not, under Roman rule, carry out the death sentence. They accused Jesus of treason, an offense warranting the death penalty under Roman law and brought him before Pilate for sentencing.

The Via Dolorosa

The Via Dolorosa is the traditional route marking the way Jesus walked from the Antonia, where he was tried, to Golgotha, where he was crucified.

Fourteen stations along the Via Dolorosa signify the events recorded in the Gospels, such as the place where Jesus received the cross, the spot where he fell, and the area where Simon of Cyrene helped the Lord to carry the cross.

Although today thousands of pilgrims walk this route, originally Jesus was accompanied by only a handful of men—two other prisoners, a centurion and a few Roman soldiers.

Each Friday at 3 P.M. a procession of devout Christians follows the way of the cross through the narrow streets of the Old City, reverently observing the fourteen stations of the cross.

Golgotha, The Place of the Skull

"And he bearing his cross went forth into a place called the place of a skull, which is called in the Hebrew Golgotha" (John 19:17).

Traditionally, Golgotha, or Calvary (from the Latin word) is located within the Church of the Holy Sepulchre. However, during the nineteenth century, this site was seriously questioned as being the authentic place.

In 1842, Otto Thenius of Dresden, a German scholar, suggested that the Crucifixion of Christ probably took place outside the north wall of Jerusalem, near the rocky knoll known as Jeremiah's Grotto. (Within the hill of Golgotha, according to Jewish tradition, is the Grotto of Jeremiah, a great natural cave where the prophet Jeremiah wrote the book of Lamentations.)

In 1883, forty-one years after this observation by Thenius, General Gordon, the noted British soldier and Bible scholar, was on leave in Palestine. He researched the death and Resurrection of Jesus Christ and became fascinated by the skull-like rock rising abruptly from the open ground north of the Damascus gate. This "skull hill" fit the description of Golgotha in the Bible. It definitely looks like a human skull (John 19:17). It is "nigh to the city" of Jerusalem (John 19:20). Jesus "suffered and died outside the city gates" (Heb. 13:12). It is near the crosscurrent of people going here and there, perhaps a highway in Christ's day. His death was visible to all who "passed by" (Matt. 27:39) and to those who watched "afar off" (Luke 23:49). This would be keeping in accord with Roman practice as described by Quintilian: "Whenever we crucify criminals, very crowded highways are chosen so that many may see it, and many may be moved by the fear of it because all punishment does not pertain so much to revenge as to example."

General Gordon's enthusiasm spilled over in the letters he wrote to friends back in England. Funds were raised to purchase the ground in front of the Garden Tomb and extending southwards to "the place of the skull." In time, the hill became known as "Gordon's Calvary."

Nat Olson

Light the candles, set the tall white lilies
High upon the altar of your heart.
Place the picture of the newly-risen
Christ above that altar—set apart
This day for worship and for glad rejoicing,
For once, before the dawn, the Christ arose,
And hope that had been crushed to earth sprang upward
More radiant than any light that glows.

Hold fast that hope, keep faith's white fire burning,
Cling close to truth, and it will make you free.
Doubt not that He who had been dead is risen
To be our light throughout Eternity.
"Because I live," He said, "ye shall live also."
Cry out the news to hearts that grope in need.
Let the glad tidings be your Easter greeting:
"The Christ is risen, the Christ is risen indeed!"

Grace Noll Crowell

Easter

From LET THE SUN SHINE IN by Grace Noll Crowell. Copyright
© 1970 by Fleming H. Revell Company. Used by permission.

Pax Vobiscum
Peace Be with You

Friend, you have come to this Church, leave it not without a prayer. No man entering a house ignores him who dwells in it. This is the house of God and He is here.

Pray then to Him who loves you and bids you welcome and awaits your greeting.

Give thanks for those who in past ages built this place to His glory and for those who, dying that we might live, have preserved for us our heritage.

Praise God for His gifts of beauty in painting and architecture, handicraft and music.

Ask that we who now live may build the spiritual fabric of the nation in truth, beauty and goodness and that as we draw near to the one Father through our Lord and Savior Jesus Christ we may draw nearer to one another in perfect brotherhood.

The Lord preserve thy going out and thy coming in.

This greeting appears in the porch
of the Cathedral Church at Chester, England

Complete Love

On top of a hill lay a rough-hewn cross.
　The man had helped bring it there;
He'd been convicted in an angry court
　In a trial that just wasn't fair.

A leather whip with metal tips
　Had been used, and His back was torn;
Blood trickled from wounds on His head
　From a crown of thorns that was worn.

His face was swollen and bleeding,
　His lips were all bruised and dry;
The people jeered, the soldiers pushed,
　All shouted, "Today He must die."

They shoved Him roughly against the cross,
　Pounded nails through His hands and feet;
A sign was added, KING OF THE JEWS,
　The words could be seen from the street.

He clenched His teeth in agony
　When the cross was dropped in its hole;
The length of His aching body
　Seemed to shiver as if very cold.

He gazed at the people beneath Him
　And cried out to His Father above;
He asked that they might be forgiven
　Because of His mercy and love.

There was a cross on either side,
　On each hung a common thief;
"We should be here, but not Him,"
　Said one who was filled with grief.

"Remember me in Your kingdom,"
　Said the same thief, now with regret;
"Today you will be in paradise,"
　The Lord replied as their eyes met.

He hung there suspended for hours
　Enduring the intense pain of the cross;
He could have been freed by angels
　But He knew mankind would suffer the loss.

"It is finished," Jesus sighed
　As He drew in His last, labored breath;
The bonds of sin were loosed from the world
　At the moment of His death.

A soldier thrust a spear in His side,
　As scripture proclaimed from the start.
Blood and water flowed from the wound
　Showing proof of His broken heart.

Yes, Jesus bore the sins of the world
　On a cross some folks call a tree;
And died to give us eternal life
　Because He loves both you and me.

Thomas D. Fender

Arisen

The women left at first light that morning,
Walking through spring flowers in bloom;
In their sadness they didn't even notice
They were rushing to get to the tomb.

They carried some sweet-smelling spices
That were used in preparing the dead.
He whom they loved had been crucified;
Ever since they had been filled with dread.

The tomb had been carved in a mountain;
A massive stone was used for the door.
When reaching the site, both were afraid
Because the stone wasn't there anymore.

Trembling, they inched their way forward
To take a closer look inside;
"Someone has taken the body," they exclaimed,
And both broke down sobbing, and cried.

An angel spoke to the two women
"I bring you greetings on this fine day.
The Lord is not here. He has risen.
Come and see the place where the Lord lay."

These words have stood throughout the years,
Bringing real hope to all who would hear.
Jesus rose from the dead as He promised;
Only believe and you, too, can share.

Thomas D. Fender

Philip

Jesus found Philip—a practical man—
And He called out saying, "Come, follow Me!"
At once Philip followed without a plan,
Walking beside Him and happy to be.
Next he shared this Christ with a friend of old,
Nathanael-Bartholomew by name.
"Come see Him of whom the prophets told!"
And Nathanael-Bartholomew came.

Still seeing that things were practically done,
Philip came along to the Upper Room.
He knew not that Christ and the Father were one
Till the day Christ arose from the tomb.

Then this practical man found the faith to employ.
He preached to them Christ and brought the world joy.

Bartholomew

Nathanael, sometimes called Bartholomew,
Philip's friend who came still disbelieving,
Soon learned that good things came from Nazareth, too,
Though years of study slowed his believing.
Born in Cana, he must have been a guest
At the wedding—walked where the Savior trod.
Long before that day Christ had passed the test,
Nathanael knew he was the Son of God.

Three years they traveled along dusty ways;
Scenes filled with miracles, blind received sight.
Twelve chosen men could speak nothing but praise.
Christ taught, "I am the way and the light."

Skeptical at first, Nathanael grew strong.
In faith he stood out far above the throng.

Thomas

Thomas, the twin, so the story is told,
Was one who doubted that Christ lives again.
"I would see for myself," he said so bold.
"I would see the nailprints that caused Him pain."
Christ, knowing his heart, appeared once more—
Came to the place where the apostles had trod,
(They had hidden away behind a closed door.)
He heard Thomas say, "My Lord and my God!"

Later they fished the Tiberias Sea
All night with no catch. When morning arose
Christ called to them, "Children, have you meat?
Cast your nets to the right." Their nets overflowed.

"Be not faithless, but believing," Christ said.
Thomas, who doubted, now believed instead.

Matthew

Matthew, business man, cash and accounting.
The least likely candidate one could choose
To be a disciple. Bad opinions surmounting,
Hadn't he often kept out more than his dues?
Jesus said to Matthew, the sinner, "Come."
He arose without question or thought.
It was a sign that no one was excluded from
This new order that Christ's coming had brought.

Jesus ate with Matthew's disreputable friends
While the Pharisees exclaimed in disgust.
He said, "I come to call men from their sins.
God is faithful, forgiving and just."

Matthew, the publican, gratefully came—
Left us the gospel that bears his good name.

The Ornamented Egg

Lorraine Wood

The egg is nature's perfect package. It has, during the span of history, represented mystery, magic, medicine, food and omen. It is the universal symbol of Easter celebrations throughout the world and has been dyed, painted, adorned and embellished in celebration of its special symbolism.

Before the egg became closely entwined with Christianity and Easter, it was honored during many rite-of-Spring festivals. The Romans, Gauls, Chinese, Egyptians and Persians all cherished the egg as a symbol of the universe. From ancient times eggs were dyed, exchanged and shown reverence.

In pagan times the egg represented the rebirth of the earth. The long, hard winter was over; the earth burst forth and was reborn just as the egg miraculously burst forth with life. The egg, therefore, was believed to have special powers. It was buried under the foundations of buildings to ward off evil; pregnant young Roman women carried an egg on their persons to foretell the sex of their unborn children; French brides stepped upon an egg before crossing the threshold of their new homes.

With the advent of Christianity the symbolism of the egg changed to represent, not nature's rebirth, but the rebirth of man. Christians embraced the egg symbol and likened it to the tomb from which Christ rose.

Old Polish legends blended folklore and Christian beliefs and firmly attached the egg to the Easter celebration. One legend concerns the Virgin Mary. It tells of the time Mary gave eggs to the soldiers at the cross. She entreated them to be less cruel and she wept. The tears of Mary fell upon the eggs, spotting them with dots of brilliant color.

Another Polish legend tells of when Mary Magdalen went to the sepulchre to anoint the body of Jesus. She had with her a basket of eggs to serve as a repast. When she arrived at the sepulchre and uncovered the eggs, lo, th[e] pure white shells had miraculously taken on a rainbow [of] colors.

Ornamenting and coloring eggs for Easter was th[e] custom in England during the middle ages. The househo[ld] accounts of Edward I, for the year 1290, recorded a[n] expenditure of eighteen pence for four hundred and fif[ty] eggs to be gold-leafed and colored for Easter gifts.

The most famous decorated Easter eggs were tho[se] made by the well-known goldsmith, Peter Carl Faberg[é.] In 1883 the Russian Czar, Alexander, commissione[d] Fabergé to make a special Easter gift for his wife, th[e] Empress Marie.

The first Fabergé egg was an egg within an egg. It ha[d] an outside shell of platinum and enameled white whic[h] opened to reveal a smaller gold egg. The smaller egg, i[n] turn, opened to display a golden chicken and a jewele[d] replica of the Imperial crown.

This special Fabergé egg so delighted the Czarina tha[t] the Czar promptly ordered the Fabergé firm to desig[n] further eggs to be delivered every Easter. In later yea[rs] Nicholas II, Alexander's son, continued the custo[m.] Fifty-seven eggs were made in all.

Aline Becker, egg designer whose work is pictured her[e,] believes in the egg's symbolism and celebrates the egg b[y] decorating it with superb artistry. Using flowers an[d] leaves from greeting cards, tiny cherubs, jewels an[d] elegant fabrics, braids and trims, Ms. Becker adorns eg[gs] she has separated with fine cutting tools. With great sk[ill] she delicately hinges and glues with epoxy and transpare[nt] cement, then covers the completed egg with a glossy res[in] finish.

These finely crafted works of art have been featured o[n] the NBC Today show and displayed at egg shows acro[ss] the country. Although the omens and the mystery of th[e] egg have disappeared today, the symbolism remains, an[d] American artists continue in the old world tradition [of] adorning eggs.

Pansy egg. The porcelain-like pansy flowers which decorate this egg were cut from greeting cards. Multiple cards were cut and glued onto the egg in order to build up a three dimensional layer. Each separate flower and leaf was molded by hand to achieve a life-like curve. A finish of glass-like resin was applied to strengthen and preserve the effect. The front of the egg is hinged and drops downward to reveal a kneeling cherub inside.

Iris Egg. This goose egg has been cut and hinged to form a three petal opening. The exterior of the egg was first painted and then lightly sanded to soften the color. The paper iris flowers and leaves were applied and raised for a repoussé effect. Each cut section was edged with gold braid and hinged. The interiors of each cut section were lined with velvet. Inside the egg stands a cherub playing the flute.

Sculptured Cherubs. A commercial, low-relief cherub sculpture scene was trimmed, painted and antiqued to decorate the exterior of this egg. Velvet, fancy gold braid, and jewel drops complete the exterior finish. The cutting and hinging of this egg was traditional. It is a horizontal cut which makes the egg into an egg box, normally used to store jewelry. When opened, the interior lid displays a silk print while the bottom interior section is softly lined with luxurious fabric.

James, the Less

One of those mysteries yet to be solved
Is the disciple James, and who he was.
We know his mother was deeply involved.
She was Mary who came to the tomb because
They had spices and wanted to anoint Him.
We know James' father was Alpheus, too.
But it was Christ who chose to appoint him
One of the twelve, and gave him his work to do.

"Provide no scrip for your journey, no shoes.
Heal the sick, cleanse the leper," He said.
"Go into whatsoever town you choose—
Cast out devils, freely give, raise the dead."

Although little is known of James, the Less,
Christ saw in him faith and righteousness.

Judas, Not Iscariot

Judas, called Thaddaeus, was fine and true.
The name means "dear one" or "from the heart."
Those who walked daily so near to him knew
He was humble and loving right from the start.
Judas, not Iscariot, thus John wrote,
Being careful to show which one he meant.
So much is told of Judas, you will note,
But of the other, only one event.

At the Last Supper Christ's teaching was heard.
To Judas who questioned, came words of praise.
"If a man love me, he will keep my word—
I and my Father will love him always."

A name can mean much or nothing at all.
It's how lives are lived that others recall.

Simon

Zealots were political with one goal
To save Judea from the Roman rule.
Christ chose Simon for a different role
Where love and honor were accepted tools.
Simon, the Zealot, was a servant of God
With enthusiasm that could inspire
Others. Daily he walked the paths Christ trod
And was zealous to set the world on fire.

From the Mount of Olives to Jerusalem
Was only one sabbath day away.
Here Simon came to an upper room
And with others began to fast and pray.

A patriot, yes . . . with a different plan . . .
Gave his all for the cause of God and man.

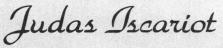

Judas Iscariot

Now Judas was hell-bent for destruction—
Bound and determined to have his own way.
One of twelve who had heard Christ's instruction,
Money was the trap that led him astray.
True, he was the tool authorities used.
The promise of money was all he asked.
He stood before Christ. It was time to choose.
One of the twelve chose that devilish task.

Repenting, he tried his best to appeal
Saying, I betrayed an innocent man.
He took his own life. They bought Potter's field.
Ancient prophets had told of the plan.

That one of the twelve betrayed Christ the Lord
Has been recorded in God's Holy Word.

MAPLE GLAZED HAM

A tempting entrée.

- 1 7 to 8-lb. fully cooked, smoked ham shank
- 1 c. maple syrup
- 2 T. cider vinegar
- 1 T. prepared mustard
  Whole cloves

Combine syrup, vinegar and mustard. Place ham, fat side up, on rack in shallow roasting pan. Pour about ½ cup mixture over ham and bake, uncovered, in a preheated 325° oven for 1½ hours. Baste every 30 minutes with additional sauce. Remove ham from oven and score fat into diamond shapes. Insert a clove into each diamond. Bake ham an additional 30 minutes or until a meat thermometer inserted into the thickest part of meat registers 140°. Let ham rest 15 minutes before carving. Makes 10 to 12 servings.

Naomi Arbit
June Turner

For many Americans, Easter dinner would be only half a feast without a tender, pink, succulent ham, and this type of pork is popular throughout the world, as well. Transylvanians bake their ham in a covering of bread dough. In Hungary it is the custom to serve an Easter meat loaf of chopped pork, ham, eggs, bread, and spices. The custom actually goes back as far as William the Conquerer, who served it along with such things as *gammon* and tansy pudding.

Some believe that ham became traditional because the pig is a symbol of prosperity in many cultures. *Schwein haben*, a popular German expression, literally means to "have a pig." At one time it was fashionable to wear little figures of pigs on watch chains and charm bracelets. Piggy banks for children may also be an expression of this age-old idea.

Easter 1895

New York's Easter Parade

Each year people gather from near and far to join in New York City's annual Easter parade. But this is not a parade in the traditional sense—there are no marching bands, baton twirlers, or even waving banners. It is a parade made up of the onlookers themselves, who come to see and be seen, strolling in their new Easter clothes down fashionable Fifth Avenue on Easter Sunday.

The origin of wearing new clothes, "Easter finery," on Easter Sunday can be traced to ancient times when the New Year began in March and people wore new clothes to signify a new beginning. There is also the belief that it originated with the early Christians who were baptized during the Easter Vigil services and wore new white robes for the occasion. The regular members of the church would also don new attire to commemorate their own baptisms.

In time the custom of wearing new garments became tied to superstition, such as the American belief that a person can ensure good luck for an entire year by wearing three new things on Easter day. From such a belief came the rhyme:

At Easter let your clothes be new,
Or else be sure you will it rue.

In any case, throughout the centuries, new Easter attire has been mainly associated with the concept of newness and a fresh beginning.

Eventually the wearing of new clothes led to the idea of parading in them. There are many Easter parades throughout this country on Easter Sunday. Some of these fashion promenades have judges to select the most appealing, or sometimes the oddest, finery. There are prizes for the best-dressed individuals or families and, traditionally, the woman wearing the prettiest hat.

The most famous Easter parade occurs in New York City. Since the mid-nineteenth century, New Yorkers and visitors alike have been flocking to the Corners of Fifth Avenue and Park Avenue to begin what has become an annual ritual. The New York Easter parade actually grew out of a tradition dating back to the first Christian settlements on Manhattan Island. Soon after the early Dutch settlers established themselves they began the custom of forming a very informal procession on Easter Sunday in what is now the Battery section of the city. Of course, there was no Fifth Avenue then. The simple townsfolk would merely stroll home from church dressed in their new spring clothes.

Later, when Trinity Church became the leading religious edifice in town, the procession formed on Broadway and worked its way uptown, recruiting from St. John's on the west, from St. Mark's and St. George's on the east, and from a number of other churches in between. It even extended as far as St. Paul's in the post-Revolutionary days when General Washington worshiped there. When Grace Church was built, it promptly became one of the major contributors to the procession.

In the years that followed, the parade became increasingly confined to the wealthier members of the city's population. It evolved into a sedate, stately affair of ladies and gentlemen wearing the most elegant and latest fashions of the day, strolling on the sidewalks or riding in horse-drawn carriages in front of St. Patrick's Cathedral. These well-dressed people enjoyed sauntering down Fifth Avenue after attending morning services in the fashionable churches of St. Thomas or St. Bartholomew. Friends would greet each other on the street and admire one another's attire.

In 1905, E. S. Martin, a well-known author of the day, acknowledged the growing concern that too much interest in clothes distracted from the religious significance of the day. He wrote in *Harper's Weekly* the following defense of New York's annual Easter event: ". . . . There is a great outpouring of flowers at Easter . . . . Every one who feels the Easter spirit and can lay hands on a flower keeps the flower in sight to show his sympathy with the prevailing sentiment. But as flowers adorn the earth, so do pretty clothes adorn the dwellers upon it, and if flowers bloom for the glory of their Maker, so may bloom the clothes, too . . . ."

Today, on Easter Sunday, after observing the appropriate religious rites of the day, New Yorkers still revel in light-hearted gaiety along the glamorous thoroughfare of Fifth Avenue. More than a dozen blocks of the avenue are closed to vehicular traffic to allow the thousands of pedestrians gathered there to walk in the street. One can still see brightly arrayed people, and sometimes, in recent years, equally adorned pets, carrying on the much-loved tradition of the annual Easter parade.

Michele Arrieh

Easter 1919

The Easter Rabbit Recommends . . .

GREEN COCONUT NESTS

An Easter treat, easy to make.

- 1 lb. green chocolate coating
- 1 7-oz. pkg. flaked or shredded coconut
  Water

In the top of a double boiler, melt coating over hot, not boiling, water. Add coconut and mix together well. Add very small amounts of water to coconut mixture until it thickens enough to hold shapes. Form into small nests by making mounds and then hollowing them out with the bowl of a spoon. Fill nests with jelly beans or molded chocolates. Makes 8 nests.

CREAMY EASTER EGGS

Excellent also for candy bars. Just pat candy into a square on waxed paper, cut into bars and dip in chocolate.

- 3 T. invert sugar
- 1/3 c. chopped candied cherries and pineapple
- 1/3 c. chopped walnuts or pecans
- 3 c. sugar
- 2 T. light corn syrup
  Dash of salt
- 1/2 c. water
- 1/2 t. vanilla
- 1 c. plus 2 T. marshmallow creme
  Dipping chocolate

In a small saucepan, combine invert sugar, fruit, and nuts. Stir and boil 2 to 3 minutes; drain, reserving liquid. Combine liquid, sugar, corn syrup, salt and water in a 2-quart saucepan. Cover tightly, and bring to a boil. Uncover and place thermometer in pan; cook to 250°. Pour candy out on a marble slab and cool to lukewarm. Work candy with a spatula until it is opaque. Add vanilla and marshmallow creme. Continue to paddle candy until creamy. Add prepared fruit and nuts; knead into candy. Form into egg shapes and let stand for a couple of hours. Dip in chocolate. Makes 16 medium-size eggs.

FRUIT AND NUT EASTER EGG

This can be made long before needed. Improves as it ripens.

- 2¼ c. sugar
- 1 c. light corn syrup
- ¾ c. hot water
- ½ lb. marshmallow creme
- ½ c. shortening, melted
- ¼ c. confectioners' sugar
- 2 c. candied fruit (cherries and pineapple)
  Nuts
  Dipping chocolate

In a saucepan, cook sugar, syrup, and water to 265°. Add marshmallow creme and beat until almost firm. Add melted shortening, confectioners' sugar, candied fruit, and nuts. Mix well, shape eggs by hand and dip. Will keep 6 to 8 months. Makes 10 eggs.

SUGARED MARSHMALLOW BUNNIES AND CHICKS

This chewy marshmallow can be formed in any mold.

- ¼ c. water
- 3½ T. plain gelatin
- ¼ c. water
- 1¼ c. sugar
- ¾ c. invert sugar
- ⅜ c. light corn syrup
- ½ t. vanilla
  Flavoring and coloring, if desired
  Colored sugar

In a mixing bowl soak gelatin in water. In a saucepan, combine water, sugar, and invert sugar. Heat but do not boil; pour hot syrup into gelatin, beating slowly. Gradually add corn syrup and vanilla, beating on medium-high speed of mixer until mixture is fluffy, white, and doubled in bulk. Color and flavor marshmallow as desired. Keep mixing bowl in a larger bowl of very hot water to keep marshmallow from hardening. Butter Easter molds and spoon candy into molds. Set aside about 1 hour; remove from molds and roll in colored sugar. Dry candy for a few hours, then pack in tightly covered containers. Makes 12 to 15 molds.

For more candy recipes we suggest
Ideals Candy Cookbook.
Recipes courtesy of Mildred Brand.

John Newton

John Newton, born in London, England, in 1725, came to be a much revered minister and hymn writer, but there was nothing exemplary about his youth. Although his mother gave him some religious training, she died of tuberculosis when he was only seven. He received little formal education before going to sea with his father, the commander of a merchant ship, at age eleven. In 1743, he was forced to serve aboard the H.M.S. Harwich, and soon deserted. He was captured, flogged, and degraded to a common seaman. After asking to be exchanged to a slave ship, he suffered brutal persecution before being rescued by a friend of his father. Newton later said that in the course of these wanderings he lost all sense of religion. But, during a severe storm on the homeward voyage, he experienced a strong religious conversion. Upon his return, Newton married a childhood sweetheart. For a time he commanded a slave ship, attempting to repress the swearing and immoral conduct of his sailors, and reading Liturgy twice each Sunday with the crew. He also successfully educated himself, learning Euclidean geometry, Latin, Greek, Hebrew, and Syrian. When he first applied to be ordained, he was refused, but later became curate of Olney, a small market town. Here he became good friends with the poet William Cowper, and the two collaborated on the *Olney Hymns*, which they stated were "for the use of the plain people." In 1780, Newton moved to London and continued preaching until the end of his life in 1807, although during the last years he became so blind he could not see his text. Newton is best known for his hymns; particularly popular today is "Amazing Grace." In his time, he was appreciated for a book of his early life and religious experiences, and for his religious correspondence. His strong conviction and his direct approach to mankind's temptations and troubles gave his work lasting appeal.

Glorious Things of Thee Are Spoken

Glorious things of thee are spoken,
Zion, city of our God;
He whose word cannot be broken
Formed thee for His own abode.
On the Rock of Ages founded,
What can shake thy sure repose?
With salvation's walls surrounded,
Thou mayst smile at all thy foes.

See! The streams of living waters,
Springing from eternal love,
Well supply thy sons and daughters,
And all fear of want remove.
Who can faint when such a river
Ever flows their thirst to assuage—
Grace, which, like the Lord the Giver,
Never fails from age to age?

Blest inhabitants of Zion,
Washed in the Redeemer's blood,
Jesus, whom their souls rely on,
Makes them kings and priests to God.
'Tis His love His people raises
Over self to reign as kings;
And as priests, His solemn praises
Each for a thankoffering brings.

Saviour, if of Zion's city
I, through grace, a member am,
Let the world deride or pity,
I will glory in Thy name.
Fading is the worldling's pleasure,
All his boasted pomp and show;
Solid joys and lasting treasure
None but Zion's children know.

May the Grace of Christ, Our Saviour

May the grace of Christ, our Saviour,
And the Father's boundless love,
With the Holy Spirit's favor,
Rest upon us from above.

Thus may we abide in union
With each other and the Lord
And possess, in sweet communion,
Joys which earth cannot afford.

Safely through another week,
God has brought us on our way;
Let us now a blessing seek,
Waiting in His courts today.
Day of all the week the best,
Emblem of eternal rest!
Day of all the week the best,
Emblem of eternal rest!

While we pray for pard'ning grace.
Through the dear Redeemer's name,
Show Thy reconciled face,
Take away our sin and shame.
From our worldly cares set free,
May we rest this day in Thee.
From our worldly cares set free,
May we rest this day in Thee.

Here we come Thy name to praise;
May we feel Thy presence near.
May Thy glory meet our eyes,
While we in Thy house appear.
Here afford us, Lord, a taste
Of our everlasting feast.
Here afford us, Lord, a taste
Of our everlasting feast.

May Thy gospel's joyful sound
Conquer sinners, comfort saints,
Make the fruits of grace abound,
Bring relief for all complaints.
Thus may all our Sabbaths prove,
Till we join the Church above.
Thus may all our Sabbaths prove,
Till we join the Church above.

The Name of Jesus

How sweet the name of Jesus sounds
In a believer's ear!
It soothes his sorrows, heals his wounds,
And drives away his fear!

It makes the wounded spirit whole
And calms the troubled breast;
'Tis manna to the hungry soul,
And to the weary, rest.

Dear name! The rock on which I build,
My shield and hiding-place,
My never-failing treasury, fill'd
With boundless stores of grace—

By Thee my prayers acceptance gain,
Although with sin defiled;
Satan accuses me in vain,
And I am own'd a child.

Weak is the effort of my heart,
And cold my warmest thought;
But, when I see Thee as Thou art,
I'll praise Thee as I ought.

Till then, I would Thy love proclaim
With every fleeting breath;
And may the music of Thy name
Refresh my soul in death!

Amazing Grace!

Amazing grace! How sweet the sound
That saved and set me free!
I once was lost but now am found,
Was blind but now I see.

'Twas grace that taught my heart to fear,
And grace my fears relieved.
How precious did that grace appear
The hour I first believed!

The Lord has promised good to me,
His word my hope secures.
He will my shield and portion be
As long as life endures.

Through many dangers, toils, and snares,
I have already come.
'Tis grace hath brought me safe thus far,
And grace will lead me home.

America's First Capital
Williamsburg

Two hundred years ago Williamsburg, Virginia, a small tidewater town, nurtured the men and ideals that led the colonies to declare their independence and create a nation.

It was here, in the capital of England's largest colony in America, that George Washington, Thomas Jefferson, Patrick Henry, George Mason and the Lees reached political maturity. It was here that they and other Virginia leaders initiated the call for the Declaration of Independence.

Today the old city has been preserved and restored to its era of greatness by John D. Rockefeller, Jr. It appears much as it did when Patrick Henry thundered his defiance of King George III and the Virginia burgesses voted their historic resolution for independence.

Reflections of those momentous days still live in Williamsburg. The historic area today encompasses 173 acres, and within it and its immediate surroundings there are 88 original eighteenth- or early nineteenth-century houses, shops, taverns, and public buildings.

Another 50 major buildings and many smaller structures have been rebuilt on original sites. Approximately 90 acres of gardens and public greens provide an authentic setting for the restored eighteenth-century capital.

Colonial Williamsburg is open to the public 365 days a year and offers up to 40 different activities on varying daily and seasonal schedules. There are numerous opportunities for visitors to tour the historic area. Exhibitions include the Capitol, Raleigh and Wetherburn's taverns, Magazine and Guardhouse, Public Gaol, Brush-Everard House, James Geddy House and Silversmith Shop, the Courthouse of 1770, the homes of patriots Peyton Randolph and George Wythe, the James Anderson House, featuring the contributions of archeology to the restoration process, and the Governor's Palace.

Artisans work at their ancient trades in twenty craft shops, using tools and methods employed 200 years ago. Costumed hostesses, hosts, guardsmen, gaolers, and other guides, describe and interpret demonstrations of the fine craftsmanship of the blacksmith, bootmaker, gunsmith, printer, musical instrument maker, wigmaker and wheelwright. In addition, they relate the city's history and interesting facts about various colonial residents.

Events vary with the seasons. Some visitors prefer summer, with the pungent smell of black gunpowder surrounding a muster of the costumed militia company. These same folks may trail along behind the fife and drum corps during a summer parade or ride in horse-drawn carriages through vintage streets. Others enjoy candlelight concerts in the fall or in-depth special-theme seminars held from January through the middle of March.

In Williamsburg the month of April is filled with music and flowers, along with the commemoration of Easter. Candlelight concerts of eighteenth century music are performed at the Governor's Palace by costumed musicians, continuing through May.

The Annual Williamsburg Garden Symposium features authorities speaking on horticulture, gardening and landscape design. During Garden Week, which follows, private homes are opened to the public, with candlelight tours in the evening. Visitors are also encouraged to attend Easter Sunday morning services at Bruton Parish Church.

Even the city's name and its layout hold historical significance. Williamsburg became the second capital of Virginia in 1699, replacing Jamestown, the first permanent settlement in the new world. The Virginia Assembly selected Middle Plantation and renamed it Williamsburg in honor of the reigning monarch.

The new city already held one distinction. In 1693 a royal charter had been granted for a college to be named in honor of the British sovereigns.

The royal governor and the Assembly carefully set about raising a new and well-ordered city, one of the first planned cities in America. An old horseway running the length of the settlement was straightened, widened and retitled the Duke of Gloucester Street. At the east end, the first government building in America to be given the dignified name of Capitol was erected. Midway between the College and Capitol, a residence for the royal governor was completed about 1720. This mansion became known as the Governor's Palace.

During the Civil War, federal troups occupied the area for more than two years. War and peace both took their tolls on the once-proud city, where much of the course of revolutionary history was charted. Fires, alterations and "progress" almost obliterated the treasures of the former capital.

Yet, many weathered old landmarks managed to survive into the twentieth century. In addition, through the efforts of Dr. W. A. R. Goodwin, then rector of Bruton Parish Church, John D. Rockefeller, Jr., became interested in the restoration of the entire town to its eighteenth century appearance.

In 1926 the first steps were taken to preserve and restore the city's historic area. Williamsburg, today, is a twentieth-century adventure in restoration and an exciting representative of our American heritage.

Beauty

Beauty is an all-pervading presence. It unfolds to the numberless flowers of the spring; it waves in the branches of the trees and in the green blades of grass; it haunts the depths of the earth and the sea, and gleams out in the hues of the shell and the precious stone. And not only these minute objects, but the ocean, the mountains, the clouds, the heavens, the stars, the rising and the setting sun all overflow with beauty. The universe is its temple; and those men who are alive to it cannot lift their eyes without feeling themselves encompassed with it on every side.

Now, this beauty is so precious, the enjoyment it gives so refined and pure, so congenial without tenderest and noblest feelings, and so akin to worship, that it is painful to think of the multitude of men as living in the midst of it, and living almost as blind to it as if, instead of this fair earth and glorious sky, they were tenants of a dungeon. An infinite joy is lost to the world by the want of culture of this spiritual endowment. The greatest truths are wronged if not linked with beauty, and they win their way most surely and deeply into the soul when arrayed in this their natural and fit attire.

William Ellery Channing

The Breath of Spring

The breath of spring is in the air,
　The daffodil's abloom,
With crimson tulips bright and fair,
　In springtime's sweet perfume.

The rolling fields of verdant green,
　Full rich with promise lie
Caressed by sunlight's golden sheen
　Beneath a sapphire sky.

The fairy wand upon the trees
　Has opened to the sun;
The wee brown buds, kissed by the br
　A miracle, each one.

The little birds that joyfully sing
　Their hymn unto the dawn
Are bidding welcome to the spring . . .
　And lo, the winter's gone.

Mary M. Forman

Easter . . . the time of awakening
　Before your wondering eyes,
Yesterday 'twas gray and drear
　But today a colorful surprise!

Easter

Easter . . . the time of joy and rebirth,
　You can see it everywhere,
In the crimson tulips swaying,
　In the lily pure and fair.

Easter . . . the time of refreshment,
　You can sense it in the air,
The fragrance of the daffodil
　Unfolded with tender special care.

Easter . . . the time of renewing,
　When the feeling of love abides,
The song of a bird speaks cheerfulness
　And friendships securely are tied.

Ruth H. Underhill

Walk in the Garden at Easter

Come, walk in the garden at Easter
And see the lilies in bloom.
Recall how our Crucified Savior
Stepped forth from the depths of the tomb.

In the chaliced heart of the lily
Rests a crown that is lovely to see,
Not unlike the crown which the Savior
Will wear through Eternity.

The lilies were there all about Him,
Supporting Him all through the night.
They, too, had conquered the darkness
As they rose with the coming of light.

In the beauty of springtime flowers,
Feel the tug that is light and is life.
The cross and the crown have new meaning
In the spring when the lilies are rife.

Come, walk in the garden at Easter,
Your life and your light to renew,
For the gardener who cares for the lilies
As tenderly cares for you.

Minnie Klemme

The Flowers of Easter

They have come back to field and hill,
To garden and to wood,
The crocus and the daffodil,
The violet in her hood,
The mignonette, the pansy blue,
The lily straight and tall—
So like the flowers, dewy, still,
In that old garden on a hill,
The first Easter of all!

I think the light that morning fell
In the same lovely way
On petal, leaf, and lifting bell,
As the light falls today;
That violets looked gently up,
Hearing the dawn-wind's call,
And dew was in a crocus cup
And fragrance in a lily cup,
In that old garden long ago,
The first Easter of all.

Nancy Byrd Turner

May Basket

Rise with the sun on a balmy morn,
Be off to the shaded brook!
Gather, but quickly, some violets
And snowdrops that hide in a nook.

Trailing arbutus, forsythia,
All add that special touch,
Tucked in a basket, not very large,
For someone I like so much!

On your doorknob it hangs, blossom bright.
Now to slip quickly away!
Soon you'll awaken and open your door
To find my spring basket . . . and May!

Lolita Pinney

God's Corner

The delicate fragrance of Easter lilies! The roll and ebb of resonant organ music! The stirring cadences of the velvet-tongued man of God as he interprets the Easter message! The dramatic crescendo of the choir as it rises to a climax in a final "He is risen!"

The congregation stirs. The spell is broken. The Resurrection has been commemorated for another year. One passes on to more mundane matters.

For nature, the resurrection is less dramatic but perhaps more meaningful. By the third week of the new year, ravens and owls appear in pairs in the forest. They are searching for suitable trees in which to build their nests. They are very selective in their choice. Ravens usually build in pine trees. Owls prefer the hardwoods—crotches of yellow birch or maples. By late February or early March new life erupts in those nests, and the resurrection of spring is on the way.

Another sign of nature's restoration of vigor is found at the base of trees. There may be three or four feet of snow on the ground and temperatures may be freezing, but gradually at the base of a tree the snow begins to recede. Says the forester, "That means spring is on the way." And what is spring but the resurrection of nature?

One of the most subtle indications of early change in nature's thinking is a gray shadow that appears on snow-covered areas. It is as though the heavens had sprayed dust with a lavish hand. Underneath those gray areas water is building up that before too long will surface. Shelley knew whereof he spoke when he concluded his ode to the west wind with, "O wind, if winter comes, can spring be far behind?"

Where do you and I stand in this matter of resurrection? Are we living in a rut that is slowly engulfing us? Are we steeped in traditional yesterdays? Or are we joyously living the resurrection in our daily lives because we are teeming with resurrected thought?

If we were to define "resurrected thought" would it not be thought that was revitalized by the strength of an unshakable faith in the omnipresence and omnipotence of the Father within us? Compromise is a popular fallacy. Resurrection is the lifting of consciousness from the tomb of lost hopes to the aliveness of spiritual entity.

Do we not mistakenly associate the Nazarene carpenter only with his resurrection from the tomb when in reality his entire mission was one of resurrection? His directives were simple and yet replete with restoration of vigor: "Take up thy bed and walk;" "Lazarus, come forth:" "Go, and sin no more;" "Be of good comfort, thy faith hath made thee whole."

What an influence for good you and I could be in a world sadly in need of good, were we to release the pent-up repressions that torment us and instead, rejoice in the peaceful security of a renewed and revitalized consciousness. That would be our resurrection.

Gertrude M. Puelicher

Ideals' Pages
from the Past

On the following pages
we are presenting a selection
from Spring Ideals 1949.

The Miracle of Spring

Ethel Colwell Smith

The miracle of Spring may come
    to any man on earth,
And tranquil thought may thrill with
    Life's abundant power and worth.

The sap climbs up. The tallest tip
    awakes with graceful glee,
For April's wholly unconcerned
    with laws of gravity.

Fragrant flowers are loveliest
    at close of winter's storm.
O blessed fact: No fall seed died,
    it grew and changed its form.

Then why art thou cast down, O soul,
    why not let hope hold sway?
For crucifixion always ends
    in a resurrection day.

The hour is come for thee to live
    as the son of God should live;
To satisfy the Christ within;
    to know, and be, and give.

And should some boastful bluster
    corner thee in dusky tomb,
Three days good work will raise thee
      up.
    Life needs a radiant room.

God's promises are kept. O soul,
    why not look out, and sing:
"My God is Life, and Life is mine,
    sweet certainty of Spring!"

Copyrighted and used by
permission of the author.

Spring's in the Garden

Marion Doyle

Spring's in the garden!
  Haven't you heard
Her footfalls as light
  As the breath of a bird?
Footsteps that sound
  Like the patter of rain,
Muted and merged
  With a leafy refrain;
Footsteps that hesitate,
  Tenderly linger,
Light as the touch
  Of a Chaminade's finger;
Prodding the crocus
  And hyacinth up,
Spilling the gold
  From each daffodil cup.
There! get a glimpse
  Of her pink petticoats —
They cost Father Winter
  A few silver groats!
Good gracious! she's
      hanging
  Them up on our trees
In the orchard — to dry
  In the sweet April breeze.

Oh, Spring's in the
      garden:
  I've heard and I've
      seen —
And the whole place is
  fragrant
  And misty—and green!

Copyrighted and used by
permission of the author.

Memories

I wonder if the little path
  Still winds across the sod —
The little, narrow, beaten path
  Where friendly feet have trod,
I wonder if the trumpet vine
  And flowering almond tree
Are blossoming along the way
  Just where they used to be.

I wonder if small children's feet
  Are eager still to climb
The old board fence and "cut across,"
  As long ago did mine,
And if the same old kitchen door
  Is standing open wide,
Where eager eyes may catch
  A glimpse of mother's face inside.

Oh, little memories like these
  Come creeping in betimes
And sing themselves to little tunes
  And set themselves to rhymes.
Just haunting little memories
  That seem to cling and guide
The thoughts along to open doors
  And mother's face inside.

Someday I'll find another path
  Where friendly feet have trod,
That's leading down the valley road
  And o'er the hills to God.
When on those strange eternal shores
  The heavenly gates swing wide,
'Twill just be "Home Sweet Home"
    Once more
With mother's face inside.

Our sincere thanks to
the unknown author.

Lack of initiative is due either to unwillingness to investigate and improve, for fear of giving more than one is paid for, or it is due to the "settling down" habit. Neither makes for advancement or permanent employment.

—Dr. Thos. Tapper

❦

Modern business rewards deeds and not mere words. It must get today's tasks done while it is planning for those of tomorrow.

—George M. Verity

❦

The talent of success is nothing more than doing whatever you do without a thought of fame. If it comes at all, it will come because it is deserved, not because it is sought after.

Longfellow

❦

No one ever would have crossed the ocean if he could have gotten off in the storm.

—Kettering

❦

It is the minute of talk after the hour of thought, the ounce of effort after the hour of preparation, that brings the business into the harbor of success.

—Calpet Mission

❦

Some people give up their designs when they have almost reached the goal; others push over to a victory by exerting, at the last moment, more vigorous efforts than ever before.

—Art Sisson

❦

Doing a job is like shaving, the longer you put it off, the harder it is to do.

—Martin Vanbee

We have received several requests from our readers asking for back issues of Ideals. With that in mind, we have listed the back issues of Ideals which are currently available. We trust this will allow you the opportunity to complete your personal library or order as a gift for any occasion. Write: Ideals Publishing Corporation, Dept. 102, 11315 Watertown Plank Rd., Milwaukee, Wisconsin 53201. Include just $3.00 for each title ordered. Postage and mailing will be included in this price.

SPECIAL HOLIDAY ISSUES

Easter Ideals '77
Easter Ideals '78
Christmas Ideals '78
Easter Ideals '79
Mother's Day Ideals '79
Thanksgiving Ideals '79
Christmas Ideals '79

POPULAR FAVORITES

Carefree Days Ideals '79
Homespun Ideals '79
Autumn Ideals '79

COLOR ART AND PHOTO CREDITS
(in order of appearance)

Front Cover, Fred Sieb; inside front cover, Gerald Koser; Spring in the forest, Freelance Photographers Guild; Crocus and Adonis, H. Armstrong Roberts; Old Mill at Stone Mountain, Georgia, Fred Sieb; Mother and child gardening, Freelance Photographers Guild; Baby ducklings, Alpha Photo Associates; Children dyeing eggs, Freelance Photographers Guild; Farm scenic in spring, Coon Valley, Wisconsin, Ken Dequaine; Evening primrose and sand verbena on desert along the Colorado River near Bullhead City, Arizona, Josef Muench; Norman Vincent Peale, Helen Marcus; Still life with lilies, Bibles and candles, Fred Sieb; Church with blossoming trees, Westfield, New Jersey, Gene Ahrens; La Laguna Christ of San Francisco, Tenerife, Spain, Colour Library International; Soldier viewing crosses on hill, Peter Bianchi; Stanford University Memorial Church windows, San Francisco, California, Colour Library International; Iris egg, Pansy egg, and Sculpted Cherubs egg, Aline Becker; Easter dinner, Gerald Koser; Easter candy, Gerald Koser; Governor's Palace, Williamsburg, Virginia, Fred Sieb; Spring flowers, Fred Sieb; Basket of flowers, Colour Library International; Inside back cover, Jerry Kiesow; back cover, Alpha Photo Associates.

ACKNOWLEDGMENTS

APRIL GARDENS by Grace Noll Crowell. Copyrighted. Used by permission of Reid Crowell. SPRING IS HERE by Walter Edmund Grush. From FALLING LEAVES by Walter Edmund Grush. Copyright © 1979 by Walter Edmund Grush. Published by Dorrance & Company. THE DELICATE FRAGRANCE OF EASTER LILIES . . . by Gertrude M. Puelicher. From EXCLUSIVELY YOURS, April 1974. Used by permission of the author. THE FLOWERS OF EASTER by Nancy Byrd Turner. Copyrighted. Used by permission of Melvin Lee Steadman, Jr. SPRING TODAY by Helen Welshimer. From her book: SHINING RAIN. Used through courtesy of Mildred W. Phillips. Our sincere thanks to the following author whose address we were unable to locate: Ruth Carrington for EASTER IS A BLESSING.